THE SECRET GARAGE

Unlock a Purpose-filled &
Powerful Life Through Prayer

PHIL ROBBINS

Published by:
Prime Concepts Group Press
www.PrimeConcepts.com

ISBN: 978-0-9979482-0-2

Library of Congress Control Number: 2016950970

About the Author

Phil Robbins is a lover of Jesus, a lover of people, and a lover of all things motorsports. He is also husband to Sarah, father to Gabriel, and the owner of several international businesses. He is an ordained pastor with a unique gift for bringing the gospel into business.

Phil's heart is set on helping men grasp their full potential in Christ, so they can be effective in their roles as men, husbands, fathers, and spiritual warriors.

Learn more and get connected at PhilRobbins.Com.

This book is dedicated to my Savior, Jesus Christ; my beautiful wife, Sarah; and our firstborn son, Gabriel. I'm so thankful for the power of prayer in our lives.

CONTENTS

FOREWORD
BY SARAH ROBBINS

I was broken. I felt alone. I was afraid.

On the outside, I had everything. I was leading a large sales organization, breaking records and earning great accolades. But I was hurting inside.

I had recently gone through a trial in business and a tragedy in my family. I suffered silently, because as a leader, that's what you do, right? Or so I thought.

I remember returning home one day, feeling alone, in tears. Walking through the garage to enter our home, I noticed hundreds of notecards on the walls. Notecards with scriptures on them, prayers, and declarations. The scribbles were in my husband's handwriting.

As I looked closer, I saw prayers that Phil had written about me. Prayers that I would be healed, that I would have confidence in who I was in Christ, that I would be able to forgive and be free.

I fell to my knees and cried—grateful for a husband who stuck by me in the hard seasons of life and clung to our faith when I was too weak to hold on. I knew he was warring for me behind the scenes, in steadfast prayer. This is true love. This is the power of a praying husband.

My Secret Place

He that dwelleth in the secret place
of the most High shall abide under
the shadow of the Almighty.

— Psalm 91:1, *KJV*

I love cars, trucks, and basically anything with an engine. So of course, I love garages. My favorite room is my garage. I typed most of this book there. Some people fight on the battlefield, some fight in classrooms, some fight for freedoms in courts; I fight in my garage.

You might say that my garage is my "secret place of the most High." It's where I keep my list of goals, specific prayers, and Scripture passages that God is using to call me on. On the other hand, "the secret place of the most High" can be anywhere, because God is everywhere.

Psalm 91 is one of my favorite scriptures. I pray and declare this prayer multiple times a day. It is a prayer of protection. It tells me that wherever I am—in a city I know well or some foreign port—and whatever is going on around me, I can be with Christ. There, "under the shadow of the Almighty," I am hidden from anything that could harm me—physically, emotionally, or spiritually. "He is my refuge and my fortress: my God; in him will I trust" (verse 2).

The one thing we need to make sure of in our prayer is that it aligns with God's Word. We cannot be out in the world submitting to our fleshly desires and expect God to bless us. "Take delight in the Lord," Psalm 37 says, "and he will give you the desires of your heart" (vs. 4). That's why I post Scripture quotes in my garage, next to my prayer requests.

My prayer is that all who read this book will have an encounter with the true God. I pray that you will find what the Lord has for you to do and become while living on earth. I believe that Christ wants to empower you to follow your dreams and the desires he's put in your heart.

Perhaps you wonder if Christ even has a plan for you. I know he does; God has a plan for each of us. He wants to reveal that plan to you, but most of all, he wants to reveal himself to you. Maybe you already know the Lord Jesus Christ, but he is always ready to reveal himself to you in new ways.

Prayer can change anything that is standing in the way of your entering into your destiny on earth. The power of the Holy Spirit, the power of love and understanding, will allow you to have full and true peace in anything God calls you to do.

Please follow me on my journey and take notes as you read. Ask yourself, what does God want of me? Am I fulfilling God's plan? These tough questions can start a conversation between you and the King of Kings, the one true friend who "sticks closer than a brother" (Proverbs 18:24).

* * * * *

Lord, I long to dwell in your presence. Please draw me into deeper union with you. Guide me along the paths you have for me. Amen.

CHAPTER 1

God Has a Plan

The heart of man plans his way,
but the Lord establishes his steps.

— Proverbs 16:9, *ESV*

Who am I? Philip Robbins is my name. But more than that, I am a son of God, a sinner redeemed by the precious blood of my Lord Jesus Christ.

The road to recognizing that identity has been a long and sometimes frustrating one. I have learned the power of prayer through some hard times. I have grown the most in my hardest moments.

For many years, I struggled with the plans God had for me. I figured my plans were better than his, or at least more fun. I used to say, "I'll become a Christian when I'm forty."

I am high energy and have always had an insatiable passion for life. In my younger years, this came off as a diagnosis of ADHD, the hyper kind. I'm sure I was a massive trial to my parents' faith some days. They had to look past my behavior and focus on the promises that God had given them for my life.

My parents are firm believers in Jesus and all of his promises, seen and unseen. My dad would speak God's promises behind the scenes, and when the Holy Spirit gave him a window to speak to me about something, he always did so with love. He backed up his words with his actions, to the best of his ability.

My parents' constant declarations over my life paid off. I bet if you asked them today if it were all worth it, they would say yes. I bet they would also say that these challenges helped them grow in the Lord, way more than they ever thought possible.

The Lord showed himself to me many times throughout my teens and into my twenties. I avoided many traps that the enemy set to try and steal from me the plan and purpose of God. Deep down there was a conviction in my spirit that kept me on the road toward the purpose God had for me.

Many godly men came up to me at different times, sometimes out of nowhere, and shared a word that the Lord had impressed on their hearts. And my spirit would leap inside. I know now that these words aligned with the destiny and purpose that Christ has for my life. It seemed that the Lord was establishing my steps even when I pushed back and tried to handle things on my own.

Now I know that a true relationship with Christ is the most exciting and purposeful relationship on the planet. Submitting my life to him and allowing him to mold and shape me into a mighty warrior and tender man is an amazing, ongoing process. I wouldn't trade it for anything.

That said, what is God's plan for your life? I can say that if you allow Christ to invade your life, to share with you his plans, and to throw some jet fuel on the fire, then you can stand back and watch the blessings happen. Let God establish your steps. He has the perfect plan for your life.

The Lord has a purpose for each and every one of us, and he is continually pursuing that purpose. Our job is to team up with him, so that his purpose for our lives and our desire to follow him collide.

* * * * *

Father, in the mighty name of Jesus, I bring before you today all the areas of my life. Show me what you have created me for. Reveal your perfect vision for my life. Download to my heart the purposes that you have for me.

I submit my life before you today and ask that you would use me in mighty ways, beyond what I could ever imagine. I lay before you my plans for my life and ask that you would confirm them, destroy them, or redirect them, for the glory of your name. Amen.

Chapter 2

Let the Good Times Roll!

His divine power has given us everything we need for a godly life through our knowledge of him who called us by his own glory and goodness. Through these he has given us his very great and precious promises, so that through them you may participate in the divine nature, having escaped the corruption in the world caused by evil desires.

— 2 Peter 1:3–4

I love what Peter shares with us: We can have *good times* in our life here on earth.

What are good times? How can we have them as Christians on this planet?

"God doesn't want us to have fun in life." These words rang loudly in my head when I was a child and into my young adulthood. Many people who were not godly at all and who seemed to have everything lacked true joy and true peace. Even many Christians lacked faith, fun, self-control, success, a true relationship with the Lord. I now know that the Lord allowed me to see all this so that I could share with people that a true life with Christ is *all* good times.

When I was a young teen, I had a lot of fun every day. I was filled with joy and zeal for life. I had a three-wheeler at one point, and my brothers and I would ride it in the woods, always pushing the limits with jumping and speed. The Lord impacted my life at summer camps, where I received the power of the Holy Spirit and my prayer language (see 1 Corinthians 12:10; 14:2, 5).

I worked for my Christian neighbor, splitting wood and working on engines. (I'm a very fast learner, but only when I'm shown hands-on how to do something.) I loved to buy and fix lawn mowers and tractors, which my neighbor helped me do. I also had several odd jobs with other family friends who were Christians. The Lord had me strategically placed, I know, in order to provide a godly foundation for my life. He knew that, in my teens, I needed all the grace possible, so he provided good examples for me. These men truly loved the Lord.

As I entered my late teens, there were fewer godly men in my life. I started my first construction company and also did parking lot maintenance for a guy. Over the next three years, I learned some valuable lessons. I learned what happens when I try to create my own good times the way the world does. For the most part, it was fun; but on the inside, I wasn't happy. I hungered for more. I would listen to sermon tapes and worship CDs, but I struggled to find the passion in life that these Christians were talking and singing about.

I came to a crossroads, where I had to make some tough decisions. My mind was often racing, thinking about things I had seen and how the men in my life would make decisions. Some would pray for God's wisdom and trust him; others would say something weak like, "God's going to do whatever he wants anyways"; and some, sadly, would get high, feed their flesh, or subdue inner emotion with sex.

I tried my best to talk to God and pray, and I even waited for responses. The funny thing is, he did respond. Though I had neglected my life in Christ for a long time, the presence of God was in me still. It was like riding a bike!

I began to write and pray and listen to God's Word. I did my best to follow him over the next two years, and I experienced incredible breakthroughs.

I had to limit time with some of my friends. These were the guys who would pull me back down. "Come on, Phil," they would say. "Who are you now?" I kept praying, warring in the Spirit. God was becoming more real to me, and I was experiencing the kingdom for the first time as an adult. It invaded my life with a new peace and freedom.

A buddy invited me to a youth rally at a local church. It reminded me of summer camp, with kids jumping around, worshiping Jesus with their hands raised, not the least bit embarrassed. It was crazy, and I entered right in.

The next few years would be the best of my life. I met my future wife and started another company. I had friends who loved me for who I was and who supported the calling of God on my life. The prayer that was coming from my heart was genuine. The Lord was blessing me.

And this was just the beginning. I had even better times coming. Those hard years of going back and forth with God set me up for the most amazing ride of my life.

The ability to know who we are in Christ is huge. The power of Christ is inside each and every one of us when we accept him as our Lord and Savior. The more you read His Word and allow it to fill your heart and mind, the more understanding you will have, and the better able you will be to pray and declare His Word through the good times and the hard times.

The fact that I have gone through many issues is really quite normal. Most people have issues; it's what we do with them that counts. We can allow them to teach us and to lead us to our vision, or we can allow them to defeat us in the short term.

I'm constantly working on having the character of God. How do I do this?

Second Peter continues:

> [M]ake every effort to add to your faith goodness; and to goodness, knowledge; and to knowledge, self-control; and to self-control, perseverance; and to perseverance, godliness; and to godliness, mutual affection; and to mutual affection, love. For if you possess these qualities in increasing measure, they will keep you from being ineffective and unproductive in your knowledge of our Lord Jesus Christ....

Therefore, my brothers and sisters, make every effort to confirm your calling and election. For if you do these things, you will never stumble, and you will receive a rich welcome into the eternal kingdom of our Lord and Savior Jesus Christ. (2 Peter 1:5–8, 10–11)

The Lord is giving us a clue here to how we can have good times in our lives and keep them forever. It all starts with our calling, with our election. The enemy (Satan, the devil) will put things in our path to hinder us from walking into our greatest days. But if we do as the Lord calls, we "will never stumble" but "will receive a rich welcome into the eternal kingdom of our Lord and Savior Jesus Christ" (2 Peter 2:11). Let's write the vision and start declaring God's divine wisdom over our lives. Let's walk in knowledge, self-control, and love.

I know that my potential is just being tapped. There is much more in store. "For I know the plans I have for you," declares the Lord, "plans to prosper you and not to harm you, plans to give you hope and a future" (Jeremiah 29:11). I believe this!

What is God's plan for your life? If you allow Christ to invade your life, to share with you his plans, and to throw his jet fuel on the fire (the Holy Spirit!), then you can stand back and watch the blessings happen. Let God establish your steps. He has the perfect plan for your life.

Christ did not come to harm you, by any means. He does not want to handcuff your creativity but rather to unlock it. He came that we may have life "and have it to the full" (John 10:10). Let's make a choice today, to pray through every time—good, bad, frustrating—knowing that "if God is for us, who can be against us?" (Romans 8:31).

* * * * *

Father, I thank you for unlocking my heart. I give you my heart today and, in your mighty name, ask you to heal all of the pain and frustration that have invaded my life.

I thank you for pouring the understanding of heaven on me. Reveal to me my calling, Lord. I lay before you my life and ask you to bless me.

I thank you, Jesus, for coming to give me abundant life. Thank you for giving me the ability to pray specifically for my relationship with you, with my wife, with my kids, and with all my family. Thank you for your sovereignty over my business and my ministry.

Thank you, dear God, for your fatherly blessing, in Jesus's name, amen.

CHAPTER 3

Standing on Holy Ground

Those who live according to the flesh have their minds set on what the flesh desires; but those who live in accordance with the Spirit have their minds set on what the Spirit desires. The mind governed by the flesh is death, but the mind governed by the Spirit is life and peace. The mind governed by the flesh is hostile to God; it does not submit to God's law, nor can it do so. Those who are in the realm of the flesh cannot please God.

— Romans 8:5–8

I want to start this chapter by laying down a mindset that Paul teaches us in Romans. Having your mind in accord with the Spirit of God will allow you to have his perfect vision to pray specific prayers, to unlock the promises that the Lord has for you and for friends, family, business, neighbor, coworker, a promise, a situation—this list goes on. The Lord is continually pursuing purpose in each and every one of us. It is our job to press in and team up with him, so that his purpose and our desire to follow him collide.

We need to be very targeted when it comes to praying for things. What comes out of our mouths must align with God's written Word, which can change anything. I always start with a pad of paper, on which I write down the who, what, when, and where of my prayer request. I write God's promises right next to the thing I'm praying for. This gets me to declare the truth "behind the scenes," going straight to God's throne instead of wasting valuable time dealing with a situation in the natural world with natural understandings.

For example, if I am praying to be healed of something, I look up (or google) a scripture on healing. I write on a notecard what I'm praying for (to be healed of an ailment) and the scripture (such as Psalm 107:19–21), to remind me of God's promise to heal. I pray this scripture out loud and thank God for his healing every day.

Always pray for God's wisdom to show you the right scriptures and prayers to pray. God's plans are different from our own.

Praying for anything for an extended period of time can be trying and frustrating. I have to go back to the drawing board on occasion and really seek the Lord on what I feel he has promised me. How do these things align with his Word?

> And my God will meet all your needs according to the riches of his glory in Christ Jesus. (Philippians 4:19)

> "My grace is sufficient for you, for my power is made perfect in weakness." (2 Corinthians 12:9)

> For it is by grace you have been saved, through faith— and this is not from yourselves, it is the gift of God. (Ephesians 2:8)

No temptation has overtaken you except what is common to mankind. And God is faithful; he will not let you be tempted beyond what you can bear. But when you are tempted, he will also provide a way out so that you can endure it. (1 Corinthians 10:13)

And we know that in all things God works for the good of those who love him, who have been called according to his purpose. (Romans 8:28)

These are the facts. I encourage you to write them down. Then you can read and declare these promises over your prayer requests.

One of the hardest things to do as a believer in Christ is to remember that his Word and his promises are true and for you. How long will you hold on to God's promises? One thing to grasp—and this might be hard to wrap your mind around—is that time is a reality only in creation. "With the Lord a day is like a thousand years, and a thousand years are like a day" (2 Peter 3:8; see also Psalm 90:4). If we focus on time, we're going to get frustrated. We need to fully trust God, which means trusting in his perfect timing and his perfect will. He knows best.

Going to God with your desires will return a harvest of blessings that can only come from him. God longs to spend time with us. He wants us to share with him our burdens. When we pour out our hearts to him, telling him how we really feel, this is the most precious thing to him. He desires a relationship with us more than we do with him.

Please reach out to God while you're reading or driving or whatever. As you grow in your one-on-one relationship with Jesus and the Holy Spirit, you will begin to hear his voice, in your thoughts and in your heart. "My sheep listen to my voice; I know them, and they follow me" (John 10:27).

We are in a battle for our lives. The Lord knows this, and that's why he gave us armor.

> Finally, be strong in the Lord and in his mighty power. Put on the full armor of God, so that you can take your stand against the devil's schemes. For our struggle is not against flesh and blood, but against the rulers, against the authorities, against the powers of this dark world and against the spiritual forces of evil in the heavenly realms. Therefore put on the full armor of God, so that when the day of evil comes, you may be able to stand your ground, and after you have done everything, to stand. Stand firm then, with the belt of truth buckled around your waist, with the breastplate of righteousness in place, and with your feet fitted with the readiness that comes from the gospel of peace. In addition to all this, take up the shield of faith, with which you can extinguish all the flaming arrows of the evil one. Take the helmet of salvation and the sword of the Spirit, which is the word of God.

> And pray in the Spirit on all occasions with all kinds of prayers and requests. With this in mind, be alert and always keep on praying for all the Lord's people. (Ephesians 6:10–18)

Getting suited up in God's Word on a daily basis will allow us to conquer any arrows that are flying at us and trying to stop us from even praying. The enemy doesn't want you declaring God's promises over your family, your work, your business associates, your neighbors, and your life. Freedom will come to the diligent.

God is faithful. He hears your prayers and acts on your behalf. Take your focus off your problems and keep your eyes on him.

> Let us run with perseverance the race marked out for us, fixing our eyes on Jesus, the pioneer and perfecter of faith. For the joy set before him he endured the cross, scorning its shame, and sat down at the right hand of the throne of God. (Hebrews 12:1–2)

* * * * *

Let's pray in faith:

> *Father, I believe all the promises you have for me. I place all my prayer burdens before you, confident that you love me and have the perfect plan for my life and for all the situations for which I pray.*

> *Lord, you are mighty, beyond all imagining. I know that you will work out all things for the good, in your perfect timing, according to your perfect plan. Help me to stay firm in faith, hope, and love. In Jesus's name I pray, amen.*

CHAPTER 4

Marketplace Ministry (Praying at Work)

But remember the Lord your God, for it is he who gives you the ability to produce wealth, and so confirms his covenant, which he swore to your ancestors, as it is today.

— Deuteronomy 8:18

The Lord had been so good to my construction company, but there was one part of his amazing system that we had been leaving out. During a long ride up north, the Lord impressed this on my heart.

I had been praying for many things to happen in our growing company. I was very hardworking; I probably worked too much. I was doing all I knew how to do. But the Lord showed me that I was missing the greatest accelerator, corporate prayer.

I thought, "But, Lord, I'm praying. I'm even praying with my brother, and we're in alignment on where you want us to bring this company."

This was all good, but the Lord had more for us. He told me to start praying for each employee, for his specific destiny to be revealed. He also shared that we were to come together once a week and pray. I said to myself, "Oh, boy, this will be interesting." Several thoughts entered my mind—thoughts of failure, insecurity, and anxiety. But the Lord was going to give me the ability to do this, I knew it.

Sometimes the Lord knows that he can only make us grow if he makes us uncomfortable. This call to pray with my employees took me to a new level in my relationship with the Lord. I had to be on my game if I was going to be the leader he was calling me to be.

We started one Monday morning. We prayed with our employees for about three minutes at the shop, before we left for the day's jobs. We had been on a long road of routine repair work, and most of it wasn't fun. I laid out how I was believing in the Lord for large projects—retaining walls, multi-layered patios, and landscape constructions. After I spit this out, a new excitement hit the crew.

Within a month, we landed some of our biggest, sweetest jobs. Better yet, over the summer the Lord showed up as never before among our crew—the believers and even the atheists. In fact, most of these guys didn't believe in anything to start with, but that summer they saw many answers to the faith declarations that came out of the mouths of my brother and me. They saw God show up and answer us. They knew the Creator himself had to be behind all this.

On one particular job, I overheard one of the guys yelling, "We're at God school!" God school, I thought, wow! The Lord had not only blessed me and my company, but now our employees had seen my faith in action. I believe that, as sons and daughter of the Most High, we should have the character of our heavenly Father, and it should be noticeable.

The chatter on the jobs for the rest of that summer made for some of the best moments ever. Two years after that amazing summer, my phone rang, and it was one of the guys who had worked with us. He wanted to come and hang out at the job, just so he could be around us. "I don't want money," he said. "I just want the conversation. I miss the way you were always building me up." My brother still has contact with a few guys who worked that summer and then went out and became very successful in other trades.

God had more for us. One Monday morning, I felt the Lord say that he had specific jobs for us. Knowing that he is always right, we started praying for future clients, and once again, a flood of new work started to pour in, bringing us into new relationships.

When we came into a contract with a client, we were there to do our job to the highest standard, then move on to the next job, right? This is how I thought it was supposed to go. But the Lord had a different idea. When a person came into a contract with us—whether the person was a believer or not—we were giving God an open door to bless that person. The person gave us money to do a job, which was a blessing to us, and we in turn prayed specifically for the homeowner and the property.

One thing I love about the Lord is that he constantly pursues people, even though we don't deserve his care, even though some people don't even want to know him. He loves people so much that he can even use a landscape company to release prayer over a home or business site.

One day, we were working for a woman who, along with her daughter, was going through a very trying time. I sensed the Holy Spirit whispering to my heart that the enemy had been trying to destroy them. I thought to myself, wow, Lord, this is serious. How can you use me? I just move dirt around.

I talked this over with my brother Jon at lunch. I'll never forget that conversation. We knew that there was a spirit of oppression at this house; we could feel it. So we prayed and asked the Lord what he wanted us to do. The answer I got was to march around the house seven times, declaring the Lord's word.

I thought they would consider us crazy. Then the Lord dropped some wisdom into my spirit: "You don't have to make it weird. Just think about it as you walk around the house throughout the day, and declare a breakthrough for this family." I thought, OK, Lord, I'll do this.

Five days later, the homeowner came out to talk to me. She had just received some bad news: She had breast cancer. I'm telling you, the power of Christ came flying out of my mouth so fast, I was shocked. I said, "I break cancer off of you in the name of Jesus."

The woman was shocked too but said thank you. I told her that the Creator cared so much about her that he had us working on her house right now, so that we could pray in agreement that she would be healed. She hugged us, so grateful for what had just happened.

The job lasted a few more weeks, and this homeowner became a friend. She would bring me tea every afternoon and ask me to sit and just share with her about the Lord. I would think to myself, how am I ever going to get work done if I hang out with my customers? But this was the season the Lord had me in, and it turned out to be one of our most profitable years on record. The Lord works in mysterious ways.

I believe that the Lord has you in your exact place right now so that you can gain understanding and wisdom. Some of you might be saying, "No, Phil, I'm not in God's will for my life right now." I would say, "OK, that's fine too." It is fine as long as you recognize that you can't outrun God.

Perhaps people have told you that they're praying for you, and they drive you nuts to the point where you say, "I can find my own way; don't worry about me." My prayer for you is that, no matter where you are on your walk with the Lord, you will begin to understand that he's pursuing you. He has always loved you, and he always will love you. He sometimes puts people in your path in order to pray the crap out of your life. Or as in the case of my customer, he can use your faith to bless someone with a new revelation of who God is and how much he cares for him or her.

For others of you, God is already using you and will continue to use you. Think about how your platform can be a blessing to others. Have you prayed for your employees? Have you prayed for your boss? Have you prayed with them?

The best way to show someone the love of Christ and the true power of the cross is through your actions. People will listen to you if your actions align with your words. We are all to model Christ in this age of unbelief and distress. Look around: People are dying, and people are hurting—believers and nonbelievers, at your office or other place of business. The cry of God's heart is that we allow him to use us on a daily basis, to spread his love and mercy wherever we go.

* * * * *

Pray this prayer if you want to be used on the job:

Father, I am in your hands. Please use me for your glory.

I pray for all the people whom I will encounter in my work today. Please make it clear how you want me to serve them. Use me even in my weakness. Let your good Spirit guide me.

I especially ask for your healing, love, and light to shine on _____. In Jesus's name I pray, amen.

CHAPTER 5

Lessons in Giving

"Bring the whole tithe into the storehouse, that there may be food in my house. Test me in this," says the Lord Almighty, "and see if I will not throw open the floodgates of heaven and pour out so much blessing that there will not be room enough to store it."

— Malachi 3:10

Are you uncomfortable at church during the offering? Do you reach into your pocket and grab some cash, feeling guilty or just pressured to do the right thing? I have experienced those feelings and many more.

One of the biggest blessings for Sarah and me in our life together was learning from our pastor at the time, Ken Hubbard, the importance of tithing. God's blessing is all over it. The most important thing I learned from Ken is that tithing comes from a heart condition, not a mindset or an emotional decision.

I had always been good at giving of my time and finances, but from Ken I learned why God calls us to give. The benefits of tithing come to the giver:

"I will prevent pests from devouring your crops, and the vines in your fields will drop their fruit before it is ripe," says the Lord Almighty. "Then all the nations will call you blessed, for yours will be a delightful land," says the Lord Almighty. (Malachi 3:11–12)

This really blew me away the first time I pondered it. God himself was telling me in his Word what he would do if I would be a tither. From then on, my heart would leap when it was time to give.

Sarah and I started to pray every month over our tithes and offerings. The time we spent sitting down and going over this allowed the Holy Spirit to draw us to another level of understanding. The seasons came and went, and there were many blessings. It seemed that whenever I needed a financial breakthrough, in my business or in family life, I had the Lord's complete attention.

Sarah and I are big dreamers. We both have big hearts, and we go before the Lord boldly in this area of giving. We write down our vision and tape it to the garage door, where we can see it every day. The Lord always answers us, but it isn't always in the form we pray. It is always what we need.

We had been blessed during one fall, and the Lord had been putting a specific dollar number on my heart to give, above and beyond our tithe. What was interesting about this is that I had been praying for a specific increase in profit to buy a piece of heavy equipment, and the amount the Lord asked me to give was this exact amount. It was a crossroad. Was I going to trust that God knew my need for this piece of equipment? Was he giving me a lesson in patience? Even Sarah was a little nervous, but she agreed that the peace we experienced in prayer was a good indication that we should give the extra amount.

Within four or five months, we landed some of the largest landscaping jobs that we had ever sold. These were so big that we had to rent more machines and hire more crew just to keep up. We ended up renting the specific piece that I had wanted to buy when the Lord asked for the extra tithe. The rental fee was actually more than the amount I was willing to justify for renting. I thought that maybe I should just buy this unit.

On a rain day that week, we visited an equipment dealer to check out a few units. He had a demo in stock that fit our exact specs. Within two days, we had an almost new machine at half the price of the one we had been renting. God works in mysterious ways.

This lesson of praying specifically for an item blessed me with an amazing new zeal for life. I would share testimonies of God's goodness everywhere I went, and people were shocked at the favors God had shown me. God is an amazing partner; all we need do is invite him to come in and partner with us. His timing might be a little different from ours, but it's always the best. And he's never gone bankrupt!

As Sarah and I continued to grow in our marriage and in our business, where and how we were to give of our time and talent was always on our minds. The Lord has called us to greater obedience regarding listening to him and saving for specific goals. As we tithed and dreamed about the ministry that God had for us, it was hard sometimes not to just settle on our own decisions. We made mistakes. One good part about a life with Christ is that "in all things God works for the good of those who love him" (Romans 8:28).

Submitting our plans before the Lord is so beneficial; if only we would listen! Until we get to that point, God still works with us.

Sarah and I stuck it out, and I believe that God honored us in being tithers and listeners. Prayer has given us a lot of peace and enabled us to be in the right place at the right time.

Scripture gives us many promises in this area:

> I was young and now I am old,
> yet I have never seen the righteous forsaken
> or their children begging bread. (Psalm 37:25)

> Trust in the LORD with all your heart and lean not on your own understanding; in all your ways submit to him, and he will make your paths straight. (Proverbs 3:5–6)

> Give, and it will be given to you. A good measure, pressed down, shaken together and running over, will be poured into your lap. For with the measure you use, it will be measured to you. (Luke 6:38)

> Each of you should give what you have decided in your heart to give, not reluctantly or under compulsion, for God loves a cheerful giver. (2 Corinthians 9:7)

God loves you! He will provide for you, your family, and your ministry. Pray in faith for all that you need. Pray for wisdom about how much you should give and where you should give.

* * * * *

God, you are my loving Father. I place all my trust in you. I know that you care for me.

Please give me wisdom for where and how much you want me to give of what you have given me. All is yours, Lord, at your disposal. I am but an instrument in your hands. In Jesus's name I pray, amen.

CHAPTER 6

The D-28 Zone

All these blessings will come on you and accompany you if you obey the Lord your God:

You will be blessed in the city and blessed in the country.

The fruit of your womb will be blessed, and the crops of your land and the young of your livestock—the calves of your herds and the lambs of your flocks.

Your basket and your kneading trough will be blessed.

You will be blessed when you come in and blessed when you go out.

… The Lord will grant you abundant prosperity.…

The Lord will open the heavens, the storehouse of his bounty, to send rain on your land in season and to bless all the work of your hands.

— Deuteronomy 28:2–6, 11, 12

Have you ever read Deuteronomy 28 and really believed that all of its promises were for you? I sure hadn't. But then it was one of the teachings on a Tuesday night at my church. Each person received a sheet of paper with a declaration at the top: "The D-28 Zone."

This teaching had an impact on Sarah and me; six years later, we are still harvesting the fruit. And we believe this fruit will continue forever. Once you put God's principles in place—over your family, businesses, customers, friends, destiny—you will see daily obstacles not as things to hold you down but as challenges to propel you into the future. People will look at you and shake their heads, wondering what you did.

The Lord will set you up as his kings and queens in the marketplace. The best part is that you just tell the truth: "It was the Lord's work!" I hope this gets you so excited that you can shout while you're reading it! I hope you feel the anticipation of what the Lord can do in your life.

The season of God's provision for my family and our businesses stunned us. It came during one of the greatest economic downturns of my life. The highest gas prices that have ever hit the USA were upon us.

It was fall, and my brother Jon and I had great visions for the winter. We had prayed about our snow removal business, and the contracts were coming in.

One day we were in a store renting a piece of equipment. The owner of the store, a local businessman who owned three of the largest service companies in our area, pulled us aside. He had been watching us from afar, he said. "You are on the up and up; you guys are getting ready to soar." Then he asked some provoking questions regarding our business.

It seemed like the perfect moment to ask him if he had any winter work available for subcontracting. He thought for a moment and then answered, "Yes, but on one condition." He laid it out: We could work for him for no more than two years, because we were too good to be subcontractors.

Here was a man—I'm not sure of his beliefs—and he was speaking exactly what we had been praying for. We knew that the Lord had us in a growing season and would launch us into greatness with our own contracts. We would be the company to give work and be a blessing to many. And we would always point our success back to Christ.

This conversation pointed us to a big need in our business. How were we going to get the equipment to tackle all of the work coming our way? Jon and I talked it through and prayed for God's favor and provision. We knew that he would open even crazy doors by which we could be blessed.

We prayed one morning Deuteronomy 28:12: "The Lord will open the heavens, the storehouse of his bounty, to send rain on *our* land in season and to bless all the work of *our* hands." For me the rain was money. We had two new heavy-duty trucks, which were a big blessing. But we needed a way to pay for two brand-new state-of-the-art snowplows.

Financing on commercial equipment is always very high—the interest can be as much as 20 percent. And we were very young entrepreneurs, just trying to get established. So we didn't even consider the normal routes of financing business equipment.

We had finished a job a few months before for an amazing new customer, Stanley Stuart. We had great favor with him, as we did with most of our customers, but there was something different about Stanley. He poured some of his business knowledge into us while we were working on his job. When the job was completed, he said, "Phil, if you ever need anything, please let me know."

This statement rang loud and clear in my head as Jon and I were having lunch one day. We prayed for an open door to ask Stanley if he was willing to invest in our company. I called him and shared with him my business plan and all the conversations we'd been having with folks and the new contracts that were pouring in. He said without hesitation, "I would love to help you." He had a contract drawn up, and within a week we were proud owners of two new Boss snowplows.

Our bottom line increased by over 100 percent that winter. Our prayers for provision were flowing like crazy. My faith was growing. Christ was doing a new thing with me; I could feel it.

One day, after receiving so much good news, I was pumping diesel in my truck and a woman at the pump on the other side made a comment about business. I was so fired up about what God was doing in my business, I grabbed my "D-28" sheet, went over to her, and shared all this fantastic news with her. She told me that she and her husband were Christian business owners, and they would start applying these provision nuggets to their business. Over the next few months, she would call and say, "You're not going to believe what is happening in our business."

I'm telling you, the power of Christ is contagious. He is ready to set you and everything you come in contact with on fire.

Here is another one of my God stories, a true account of how he provided when there was no other way.

The transition to more contracts led me to seek qualified people to get everything organized, so that Jon and I could focus on the work and our employees. The financial side of running a company, with all its paperwork, was never my strong suit, so I did as does everyone else who didn't go to school to become an accountant—I hired one. My brother in-law referred me to a local accountant. I did some research, found her affordable, and hired her. The burden of paperwork was lifted off my shoulders, and I was able to focus my time on the business.

One hot July afternoon, I came home from work and grabbed the mail. I shuffled through it and stumbled on a letter from the government. I opened it, and what it said brought forth words that people I grew up around told me one should never say. How could this happen, I asked myself. I had even hired a professional for this task.

The next day I contacted my accountant. Her response was, don't worry about it, it's no big deal, we will handle it. That statement proved to be so far from the truth that I had to plead the grace of God to not react in a way that I would regret.

God says in his Word, "Righteousness goes before him and prepares the way for his steps" (Psalm 85:13). I felt like, how was this preparing the way?

I brought my frustrations before the Lord. Sarah and I together, in this unknown place of unwanted pressure, released the situation to the Lord and asked that whatever he wanted would happen. We asked that he would use this as a teachable moment and make us grow way beyond where we were.

The Lord began to speak to my heart in this season. He said that he was preparing us for something huge. His actual word was "Phil, I'm getting you ready to handle millions, and I need you to go through some things so I can have you prepared and so I can get all the credit."

I had been through some God-restructuring before. I held on tight to those words. It really was my future that I was holding on to. I would prophesy those words as a promise of provision.

I remember sitting in meetings where I felt backed into a corner, with no answers and no way out. And I would blurt out, "The only reason that I'm sitting here in this room with you and going through this is because God has such big and amazing plans for me and my family in business and ministry, and he's just laying the groundwork for us to be able to handle the millions coming our way. He wants the right people to be in place from the beginning."

The looks that people gave me were priceless. I wish we had owned I-phones back then, because I would have snapped a ton of pictures.

When all the meetings were over, we found out that, through mistakes that the accountant had made, we owed the government 50k. This was a shocker! We had no idea how we would pay this. Back then, I had my small construction company, and Sarah was teaching. We had $5,000 in the bank.

We laid this $50,000 burden before the Lord. We had to pay it within a few months, and winter was approaching. With our natural eyes, it seemed we would fail, but we held in there and declared God's Word over our life.

One other thing we had was our new home-based business, which was off to a good start. Sarah was consulting for some sales organizations as well. We had even won a few trips, including an upcoming one to Mexico. We decided we should still go, leaving our financial troubles in God's hands.

Our first day in Mexico, we received an offer to help a company grow in sales, and in turn we would receive a $50,000 bonus!

I looked at Sarah, and she looked at me, and we started laughing. We grabbed some lunch, sat down by the pool, and came up with a game plan. It was a stretch, and we knew deep down that it would be impossible in the natural realm. We also knew, however, that all things are possible with God (Luke 1:37). He was for us; he was rebuilding us. Our faith shot up to a new level that day.

We went home and put into action the plan we had come up with. Sarah pounded the pavement like crazy, exceeding what anyone thought possible in that time frame. On the last day of this 50k challenge, we were still a long way away from the required increase in sales. But with one last push, an order came in to satisfy the challenge.

Within a week, we received a check for $50,000. It was a modern-day miracle as far as we were concerned. We deposited that check with the most excitement ever and wrote a check to pay off the government.

That accounting mistake moved us forward with more steam than we ever had in our life up to this point. We saw the provision of the kingdom of heaven invading our personal space. The lessons I learned were priceless; they literally set us up to be able to handle millions of dollars in business.

The biggest lessons are not always the easiest to go through, but the returns in knowledge and strength are worth the pain. They enable you to march into your future with the power of Christ on your side, not trying to do it on your own.

Lay out your business, ministry, and personal plans before the Lord. His ways are larger and better than you can think or imagine.

* * * * *

Lord, help me to grasp the plans you have for me. When a plan seems to be dashed, help me find a way through the obstacles to the blessings you have for me.

Lord, help me be faithful to you in all my dealings with others. Help me forgive those who wrong me, aid those who need me, and appreciate those who come along-side me.

Most of all, Lord, help me keep you first in my life. You are the greatest provision, the pearl of great price (Matthew 13:46).

CHAPTER 7

Specific Prayer

Ask and it will be given to you; seek and you will
find; knock and the door will be opened to you. For
everyone who asks receives; the one who seeks finds;
and to the one who knocks, the door will be opened.

— Matthew 7:7–8

I never really knew how to pray specifically for anything until
the Lord spoke to my heart about it one day. He wanted me
to be specific about what I wanted and needed. That day, I took
all the thoughts that flooded my mind and heart and offered
them to the Lord. Learning how to pray like this over our businesses, relationships, destiny, and callings has propelled Sarah
and me into a future beyond what we could imagine.

Have you ever felt as if you were in the right place but at
the wrong time? Sarah and I moved to southern California
because we liked the thought of 70 degrees and sun. We decided to rent there and look for a place to buy. To be honest,
we hadn't prayed about it much; California just sounded like
a good idea.

We learned a lot in California. But we found it hard to con-
nect with people, and we missed our family. So after several
months, we headed back to the house we still owned in Michigan. As we unloaded the trailer and moved our stuff back in,

I knew that the Lord had a better, more creative place for us to live, and I couldn't wait to find it.

After teaching for a few years, Sarah had become involved in a skin-care business, which had really taken off. She was hitting milestones that few people achieve. I had joined her in the business full-time, giving my brick-paving business to my brother.

As to where we should live, Sarah wasn't interested in staying in Michigan. I mean, it snows in Michigan, and Sarah hates snow. I, on the other hand, like snow, and Michigan is where we both grew up and where our families were living. But more than anything, I wanted to be where the Lord wanted us. I was ready to plant roots for this next season of our lives—in Michigan or wherever. I knew that figuring out our home base was going to take God's helping hand.

A goal Sarah and I shared was to live on a lake. I sat down one day and wrote that goal on an index card, along with a few scriptures. I knew that someday we would live on a lake, but I had no idea where.

One day there came a random e-mail from a Michigan realtor about a home that was for sale on a lake, along with a few other homes that were just sweet. I remember to this day looking at the pictures and wondering if one of these beautiful homes would ever be ours. I added the pictures to my prayer card.

I would go before the Lord regularly and thank him and praise him for what he had already done in my life. But I knew there was more, and I had to be specific. Could he please consider allowing us to live in Michigan? And how about one of these houses on the lake?

The summer went by quickly. Coming into the fall, I asked Sarah if she would go look at a few houses. She agreed to go, which I thought was an open-heaven miracle happening right before my eyes.

I'm not sure how we even got on the list with this realtor. We looked like two kids. I'm sure she wondered how we could afford a home like the ones she was selling. These thoughts rolled through my head, but I didn't care. We were "under cover" people. You know, people always want to judge a book by its cover. The truth was, our business was booming, and we could afford one of these homes.

The first home the realtor showed us was crazy sweet, but we didn't care for the location. The second home was the one on the water that I had seen months before. We walked up to the door, and a tall gentleman in a long black coat opened it. Our realtor had a long black fur coat on. And in trailed us "kids," as they called us.

Our first impression was breathtaking. When we reached the upstairs, I looked at Sarah, and she was crying. I said, "What's the problem?" She said she had seen a vision of us raising kids in this home. The Lord had softened her heart.

This was crazy to me but not to God. My prayers were bearing fruit. I knew that the Lord was working on both of us.

We went home that night with our hearts open to the possibility of living in this home. We created a vision, wrote it out on paper, and put scriptures next to it. We started to pray every day that the Lord would show us if this was the place he had for this next season in our lives. We knew all his promises to us, and we praised him for the coming breakthrough in this area.

We also listed all the specific things we would need in order for this home to be ours. We put down our need for an amazing realtor with a proven track record, a believer who really loved people and her job. We put down our need that everything would go smoothly with the homeowner and there would be no problems or delays if this house was to be ours. We listed our desired interest rate and a few top banks. These were areas we prayed for every day for months.

Our first realtor couldn't handle the sale, and she backed out. This sounds terrible, but it was a big blessing. We found a new realtor named Janice who was highly recommended. She was tops in everything in her company, and she loved her clients and all the people around her. She was up on every detail, which allowed things to run pretty smoothly.

The night Sarah, Janice, and I went for the second walk-through, I realized that this sale could really happen. All our prayers were directed toward this. We tried to keep our faces straight, to not show too much interest. Then Sarah entered the room where she had seen herself caring for children. That was the clincher!

Sarah, Janice, and I went across the street to Panera Bread to chat. Janice told us that there was already an offer on the home. If we really wanted it, we needed to put in an offer that night. My mind was flooded with memories of decisions I had made under pressure, decisions that had been mistakes. Was it wise to make an offer here?

Sarah and I stepped outside for a bit and talked it over. She asked me to pray for wisdom in this decision. As soon as I was done praying, I knew, with overwhelming peace, that we were to put an offer on the house.

We were in a completely different place than with previous decisions. We had done our homework. We had been praying about this for months and had a plan in place. We weren't trying to make something happen. We experienced peace and confidence in moving forward.

Our offer went in and was accepted that night. Then began the roller coaster of dealing with the banks and waiting. It felt like the longest four months of our young lives, but during it all, we kept God's promises before us. We declared his Word over the home and knew the situation was in the Lord's hands.

One night we were praying and felt led to declare that this property would be a blessing to our friends and family, that all who entered would feel the Lord's tangible presence, that heaven would open over this home, that books would be written here, and that people's dead dreams and desires would be brought to their remembrance. This was going to be a place of restoration, a safe haven where people could regroup and grow with the Lord. This would also be an inheritance for future generations.

The waiting season was a time of many challenges. The last month of waiting—which included refaxing what seemed like the same document seven times in a row—came and went. We were very busy in our businesses, but praying for this property never stopped.

At church one Tuesday night, the pastor and his wife prayed with us. With the final push in place, there was a lot on the bank's side that could keep the sale from going through. Our pastor suggested that we stake the property with scriptures. I said, "Oh, OK." I had never heard about this before, but it made perfect sense. We took large popsicle sticks, wrote scriptures on them, and stuck them in the four corners of the property.

Sarah woke up one morning and said she felt we needed, for seven days, to go to the house, walk up and down the driveway, and declare God's goodness and blessings over the land. God had called Joshua to do the same thing, and I'm sure he got a few raised eyebrows. But on the seventh day, the walls of Jericho came down (see Joshua 6).

The walls around this house came down all right, on the last possible day that the bank could fund the deal before the homeowner could get out of it. We got a call from Janice that morning, asking that we meet her at the title company to sign the papers. "The property will be yours!"

The excitement inside of me was crazy. We showed up and signed the paperwork, smoothly and peacefully, with no last-minute surprises. The people at the title company expressed amazement at our peace and the favorable loan we received. And here we looked so young. We told them, "This is the Lord's home, and everyone who enters will be refreshed and blessed."

Sarah and I now keep a list of what we are asking the Lord for, revising it every month or so. We sit down and think about what we need: healing in our bodies, contracts for business, open doors in teaching. We write down goals as it relates to our faith, family, friendships, finances and giving, fitness and health, and in the field—in ministry and business. We ask the Lord where he wants us to serve and what he wants us to give to our church and various ministries. We pray for those goals. The list goes on the garage door, so we can keep these things in our minds and hearts.

I challenge you to write down some goals if you haven't already. Make the shift: Ask the Lord for what you want, not just what you need.

But remember, the Lord is not Santa. You need to write down your calling, then begin to pray over the areas of destiny, family, business, and friends. Maybe God will call you to go outside the box, writing some scriptures on popsicle sticks and surrounding your home with them.

I believe we're entering a new season of holy boldness. Step out with Christ and take some territory for the kingdom. Research what Scripture has to say to you about the blessings that God wants for you, even in business. Don't just fly by the seat of your pants, as I did for many years. Build a solid foundation on the Holy Word of God and the power of prayer.

Be persistent; don't give up. There are people waiting for you to succeed in life. They will be impacted through the areas in which the Lord calls you to minister. No matter where you are in life, you can ask Christ to reveal his plan. And he will.

* * * * *

Pray this if you would like the Father to personally share his plans for you:

> *Father, I ask you now, in Jesus's name, to reveal the plans you have for me. Please speak to my heart and my mind, that your plan will be clear.*
>
> *I thank you, Father, that you are for me and not against me. I thank you for pursuing my heart, and I receive today all you have for me, in Jesus's name, amen.*

Listen to God's "still small voice" (1 Kings 19:12, *KJV*). Pray continually, and declare God's Word over you and over your life.

CHAPTER 8

Praying for Purpose

Write the vision;
make it plain upon tablets,
so he may run who reads it.
— Habakkuk 2:2, *RSV*

Have you written the vision for your life? If you have never done this, it's OK. Back in the day, I used to be able to keep God's vision in my head, but now the dreams he gives me are so great that I have to write them down. I don't want to miss any of them. They form launching pads to get me somewhere faster than I ever could get on my own.

One day, driving down the road, I heard a pastor on the radio talking about "writing the vision." If God wants us to write something down, it must be important. I began to write down my "visions"—my senses of what God wanted of me—put Scripture passages next to them, and read them out loud. I would ask the Lord what he thought and then listen for him to share.

One of the great advantages we have as believers is this access to clear, unhindered vision. Christ is the quarterback who always throws the perfect pass! I have applied this to my businesses and relationships over the years. I have seen hundreds of breakthroughs—miracles even—obviously coming from the hand of Christ.

A hard season comes to mind. We encountered a huge conflict in business as well as a tragedy in our family. Looking back, I can see that the Lord wanted my roots to shoot more deeply into his truth.

At this time, Sarah and I had been praying for ministry opportunities. We knew that the Lord had some doors he was going to open. I sensed the Lord saying that Sarah and I were called to the nations, to the marketplace. Our destiny was going to come to pass no matter what.

I wrote down that vision. Waiting was tough. The Lord ordained this difficult season in order to launch us into the future with our minds fixed on him. We dug deeper and deeper into God's word.

Within a few months, we had an opportunity to go to India with one of Sarah's friends, who was part of a ministry called Angel House. I thought that I would never go to India; it truly is a tough trip. But I ended up losing that conversation with the Lord. He gave both Sarah and me a heart for the country. So the trip to India was scheduled.

I always say that where your purpose is, there you will find a new peace and also a new grace. This new grace will give you the ability to walk in your unique purpose for God, no matter how crazy it seems. Even if God calls you to an actual battlefield, his grace will allow you to carry out your calling and purpose.

Every morning and night, going to and coming from work, I passed through the side door of our garage. That was where

I stuck all the flash cards on which I had written our dreams and desires, along with the Scripture passages the Lord had given us to go with them. These were coming to pass before our eyes. Our business was growing fast. Now we even had the time and money to take this trip to India and check out what Angel House was doing there.

Then came a big hurdle. The leaders of the trip, who were the founders of Angel House, were unable to go on this particular trip. They told us they understood if we didn't want to go without them. We could wait till summer, when they would be able to go.

I had a deep conviction that we were still supposed to go. I told Sarah that, and she felt the same way. We ended up going, and it was one of the greatest mission trips we had ever been on. Everywhere we went, the Holy Spirit was rocking.

I'm very outgoing, and the seven-hour bus rides gave us ample opportunity to get to know everyone on the trip. In fact, we felt as if we had been best friends with these people for years. The amount of laughing and ministry within the group was a miracle in itself.

The Lord was preparing us for our future purpose. God is always building us, stretching us, and calling us to another level. Sometimes he uses challenges. That was true for us.

It was a Thursday, and we were headed to a city five miles south of China. We had to stop at a border crossing. I had felt amazing the whole trip, but after an hour waiting at the checkpoint, I felt very dizzy. I knew I couldn't go back on the bus, so they put me in an SUV with the city pastor and our guide, and we headed into the mountains. Sarah and I were split up at this point.

I popped some Dramamine and felt much better within the hour. Just being in the jeep with my two new "pastor friends" was amazing. There were questions flying all over. In no time we had a great conversation going about destiny and why and how we were all doing what we were doing.

We were within five miles of our destination, and the bus was probably three miles behind us. The road we were on resembled an ATV trail or even, in some places, an obstacle course. (This road was featured on a TV show called *The World's Deadliest Roads!*) The fact that we had a bus coming up behind us was amazing.

I was excited just being on this road. I know, you probably think I'm crazy, and I am. I knew no one would die; we were covered. We were all set to walk out our full destinies, and this road wasn't going to stop us.

Then the phone rang. The pastor said, "It's your wife. She ran off the bus."

I said, "There's no way. She's tough." I guess the Lord had different plans, and oh, he sure did.

We turned around and met up with the bus. Sure enough, someone had been spreading fear, saying out loud, "We're all going to die."

The trip leader had Sarah hop into the jeep with us and ride back to town. The questions were rolling back and forth again—this conversation about destiny and purpose. Then out of nowhere, a guy named Steve turned around and said to me and Sarah, "I feel that the Lord is calling you guys to do something crazy."

"OK, what is it?" I asked.

Steve said, "The Lord placed on my heart his desire for you to build a home for a hundred orphans. I'm not sure how you are to do it, but I'm sure we will figure it out."

This was our first trip to India, remember. We were just checking everything out and seeing what the Lord might have for us there. And now it was as if the Lord had all these weird events line up—my sickness and the impossible road—so that we were both in a car with these folks, talking about dreams and what we were called to do. And the Lord dropped this new vision into our spirits. It seemed daunting, to say the least. "How would we do this?" we thought.

When we got home, we continued to pray and ask the Lord about this word and the purposes that he had called us to. We felt that this was an invitation from him, and we took on the challenge. We started working out a plan toward making the orphanage a reality.

The Lord moved fast, and within eleven months the project was financed. We opened the home a little over a year later. This didn't come without struggle or strain; we met a bunch of roadblocks, along with emotions that could have stopped us. But the fact is, if Christ leads you to something, he will give you the ability to accomplish it. And he will bring you to a new level of understanding of his purpose in your life.

It is amazing to see Christ's purpose for us in action. Our ministry in India has led us into our greatest years on this planet. I truly believe that we are walking out his purpose for our lives.

I also believe that each and every one of you has a specific purpose and destiny that Christ has given specifically to you and only you. It's your job to tap into his vision by spending time with him and allowing him to mold and shape you. Nothing can hinder the call of God on your life if you are willing to bring him your plans and ask him if they align with your destiny. When the going gets tough, the tough push through to the other side. And the end result? You will be filled with peace, joy, and love.

During that time, some of our greatest prayers were answered. We moved into our home. We made great friends. Our family became closer. Our businesses were blessed. We opened two orphanages—one for boys and one for girls. My wife wrote a best seller, *Rock Your Network Marketing Business: How to Become a Network Marketing ROCK STAR*. And that was all launched during the toughest season of our life.

If you want clear direction from the Lord, pray! Write down what your desires are, and bring them before the Lord. Write the vision, that you may run with it!

I believe that God is going to explode your mind with the purposes he has for you. He will open doors that have been shut, for nothing can stand in the way of anything that he calls you to do.

* * * * *

Father, in the mighty name of Jesus, I bring before you today the areas of my life for which I feel you created me. I ask you that you would reveal your perfect vision for my life right now. Download to my heart the purposes that you have for me.

I submit my life to you today. Please use me in mighty ways, beyond what I could ever imagine.

I lay before you all that I am currently pursuing. I ask that you confirm those things that are part of your plan and wipe out those that aren't. Give me direction, Lord. In Jesus's name I pray, amen.

CHAPTER 9

Family: Our Greatest Mission

It is God who works in you to will and
to act in order to fulfill his good purpose.

— Philippians 2:13

I met my beautiful wife fourteen years ago at a youth group
meeting. Sarah had just completed a degree in elementary
education and was headed toward a teaching career. We went
with our youth group on mission trips, in our home state of
Michigan and also in Alaska. The trip to Alaska was a big turn-
ing point for me. Seeing Sarah pour out everything she had to
all the little kids we encountered made me sure that this was the
woman for me. I fell in love with her beauty and her love for
God and others. We have now been married for twelve years.

God has brought us far, not only as a couple but as pastors,
teachers, and business professionals. But this wasn't the
whole promise. I knew that God, in his perfect timing, would
allow Sarah to get pregnant. And indeed he did! We are so
grateful for our son, Gabriel, and for all the blessings tied to
being parents.

One of my prayers—at the beginning, during, and at the end
of the pregnancy—was that Sarah would suffer no morning

sickness, her body would be in perfect alignment, all vital signs would be in order, and the delivery would be smooth. We prophesied over baby Gabriel for nine months, speaking to everything in his body as he developed. We had an app that showed what was developing on the baby each week, and that app helped us know what to pray for. We declared God's Word and promises over each and every stage of his birth. I know that this child will be a blessing to generations, and I'm so excited that Christ has entrusted us with this world changer!

It is my job as a husband to speak God's Word over my wife and my child. I must impart to Gabriel a father's blessing (see Genesis 49:28). This isn't God's job; he's chosen me to do this.

It's time we stand up and take our role seriously. Let's pray for our families, fight for the promises God has given us, write down our family vision, and bring our families together in prayer. Speak God's truth over them. God has given us all the tools we need to be amazing parents, spouses, and heads over our homes.

God created each and every member of our families. He formed each in the mother's womb. He knew you, your spouse, and your children before birth.

> For you created my inmost being;
> you knit me together in my mother's womb.
> (Psalm 139:13)

> Before I formed you in the womb I knew you,
> before you were born I set you apart. (Jeremiah 1:5)

God really knows us, to say the least. And he loves each one of us, and each person we love, more than we can imagine.

> What is mankind that you are mindful of them,
> human beings that you care for them?
>
> You have made them a little lower than the angels
> and crowned them with glory and honor. (Psalm 8:4–5)

You can go straight to Jesus with all your concerns for your loved ones. This includes your concerns for the unbelievers in your life. It's his job to draw all men and women to himself.

We are in a battle. There will be days when the enemy will try to steal your joy, and it may come through someone you love. Please remember one verse, Ephesians 6:12:

> For we wrestle not against flesh and blood, but against principalities, against powers, against the rulers of the darkness of this world, against spiritual wickedness in high places. (*KJV*)

Remember who the enemy is! If he can get you wrestling in the flesh against someone, then he's got you. We have to recognize his schemes, particularly when we're battling for someone's destiny.

Isaiah 54:17 gives us confidence in spiritual battle:

> *No* weapon that is formed against you shall prosper.... This is the heritage of the servants of the Lord, and their righteousness is of me, says the Lord. (*KJV*, 2000)

The key to all of this is that we show love even when it's not deserved, even when people reject us. The ability to love will come from the time you spend praying and praising and hanging out with the Lord. He is so for you. He is aware of the deep desires of your heart, which he's put there. He wants total healing and wholeness not only in your life but in the lives of people that he has put you in a position to influence.

There are many stories in the Bible of people who stood up for others before God. Abraham prayed for God's mercy on the city of Sodom (see Genesis 18:22–33). Moses interceded for sinful Israel (Exodus 32:7–14). Nehemiah prayed for the rebuilding of Jerusalem and of God's people (Nehemiah 1:4–11). As these men took their concerns to God, their key motivation was compassion. They loved the people, the culture, the faith, with a love like God's love. This love burned in them so much that they dared to take on God.

Unlike the gods of other lands, this God would not zap them with lightning or turn them into beasts. God listened to them. Without ignoring the wrongdoings that had kindled the divine wrath in the first place, he saved at least some of the people and brought them to where they belonged.

We must try to mirror, to the best of our ability, what Jesus shows us in his written Word. We have to come to a place of sacrifice, trust God 100 percent, and remember that he has people and situations in hand, with an outcome that aligns with his Word. We hold these up to him and allow Christ to take the burdens that we are experiencing. This will allow us to be more effective intercessors, rather than being weighed down by things we can't control. The understanding, wisdom, and peace we gain by doing this is stunning.

Praying for others is a big responsibility, but it's so worth it. Lives are on the line, and it is a privilege to be called a prayer warrior of the Lord. He can trust you, and you can trust him. "I know that everything God does will endure forever; nothing can be added to it and nothing taken from it. God does it so that people will fear him" (Ecclesiastes 3:14).

God calls you his sons and daughters. Nothing can take away the destiny that he has for you.

* * * * *

Pray this prayer if you would like help from the Holy Spirit in praying for your loved ones:

Father, I praise you and thank you for showing up in my life. I thank you for caring about me and for giving me your son Jesus as a sacrifice for all my sins. I thank you for giving me power over anything that I will ever have to overcome.

Father, I come boldly before your throne, knowing that you will work on my behalf in family situations. I thank you for giving me vision from heaven to see what's really taking place. I surrender my life and the lives of my loved ones to you today. I stand on the promises that you have given me, and I pray that you would hear the cry of my heart. In Jesus's name I pray, amen.

Chapter 10

Praying for Health and Fitness

The Lord will perfect that which concerns me;
Your mercy, O Lord, endures forever;
Do not forsake the works of your hands.

— Psalm 138:8, *NKJV*

When people used to ask me if I exercised, I'd tell them, "I do crunches every day— especially Captain Crunch and Nestlé Crunch."

My younger days—days of hockey and working out—were over. I was in the big world now and could make my own decisions. I really didn't like going to the gym. I was a construction worker, so I worked out every day as it was. Little did I know that ten years of stressful schedules and fast food would catch up with me.

The Lord had been showing me a few areas I needed to work on regarding my health and fitness. First Timothy 4:7–9 inspired a system that would change my life:

Spend your time and energy in training yourself for spiritual fitness. Physical exercise has some value, but spiritual exercise is much more important for it promises a reward in both this life and the next. This is true and everyone should accept it. (*NLT*)

I had been in a season of overcoming many obstacles. It was a time of learning that I wouldn't trade for anything. The Lord was building my foundation for the future. He needed me healthy and in shape, physically and spiritually.

I submitted myself to a ministry that was like a spiritual boot camp every Tuesday night. It pushed me spiritually, beyond anything I had ever known. I also joined a physical fitness program with my wife. It felt as if three days a week I was going through basic training. I would come home whooped and think, is this worth it? Two months in, I didn't see massive muscles yet.

Persistence over the next few years set me in the exact place the Lord wanted me. I grew spiritually by feeding my heart and my mind on the Word of God. I grew in physical strength through the fitness program and healthy eating. This paid off. Sarah and I were building our business and traveling a lot, for the business and for Christian ministry. It takes physical strength to do what the Lord calls you to do. He sends us into the world so we can bless his children.

I had been praying specifically for healing of a skin issue that had popped up a few years back. It frustrated me, even as I did my best to deal with it. A topical steroid helped a lot. But I believed God wanted to heal me.

I figured that in faith I was already healed, but I would be fully healed with evidence of it on my body. I received prayer for years and declared the Word over and over, but I did not see any change in the condition. *What* and *why* were my questions. Then I realized one day, after I had received prayer, that maybe my healing was around the corner.

I was out running errands, and I stopped to pick up some vitamins from Sarah's natural path doctor. There in the waiting room was a pamphlet about all the annoying little issues people deal with, issues that doctors can't fix. I said to the woman behind the counter, "I see that you have testimonies here of people getting healing from ailments."

She answered, "Yes, this is true, but it requires a lot of personal work on the part of the patient."

I told her the areas I had been dealing with, and she told me that it was possible to heal my body from the inside out using proper food and vitamins. I was stunned. Up until that point, doctors only wanted to medicate me, not fix the real issues. I thought to myself, of course, there has to be change and sacrifice in order to walk into this healing I want.

Immediately many hesitations flooded my mind. I couldn't handle this. I would be missing out; I wouldn't be able to live a normal life. Plus, I traveled too much, often to remote places where there was only a certain kind of food.

These are the types of thoughts that enter my mind whenever I'm challenged with a decision to change. It's so easy to tell someone else to change something in order to receive a benefit, but that's not something I want to hear. Yet that day, deep down, I knew this plan was the answer to my prayer. I said, "Yes, I'll take your challenge." I drove away from that clinic thinking that I can do all things through Christ; I'm an overcomer.

Over the course of the next six months, I submitted my life to this new process. Within four months, my skin had healed all over my body. The funny part is, I also lost over twenty-five pounds. I hadn't gone into the program to lose weight; I thought I needed all I could get. The process detoxed my body of all the fast-food chemicals and medications that I had been ingesting for the previous ten years. People found it crazy to see how little I got.

Now, two years later, I am so glad I took the challenge. It has me more in tune with my body than I'd ever been. I learned how important it is to feed my body whole, good food, just as feeding my spirit with the whole, good Word of God is so important. I love the challenge of working out in the gym and the joy of seeing results. If I push myself to lift a certain amount of weight, for example, in two weeks I can lift more than I had before.

I will have to make decisions for the rest of my life regarding what I put into my body and what I feed my spirit and soul. Any pain or frustration I experience in this process gives me a better understanding of how people in general confront change. I feel more equipped to help others plug into the perfect socket of life-giving power, the power of Christ and his plans, the plans created perfectly for them.

Paul writes, "Therefore I, the prisoner of the Lord, implore you to walk in a manner worthy of the calling with which you have been called" (Ephesians 4:1, *NASB*). The definition of *implore* is "to make a very serious or emotional request to someone, to ask or beg." The Lord created each of us with a calling and a destiny. But we have to find our destiny; it won't find us if we're not looking for it.

If you know in your heart that you have an area of health that needs the touch of Christ, but it's been hard for you to take action, below is a prayer I want you to pray. Speak this prayer out loud. Picture yourself standing with your daddy in heaven and telling him about the specifics. The best part is, he's already got a solution. But speaking to him out loud will get it out on the table and start the hard process of change.

Remember, God gave me the power I needed to accept the challenge in that doctor's office, and he will give you his grace to walk into your greatest years of physical and spiritual health.

* * * * *

Father, in the mighty name of Jesus, I stand before you today as your son (or daughter). I thank you that I have the ability to come into your holy presence and share the areas of my life that need your touch. I lay before you today (write what you need physically and spiritually) _____.

I thank you, Lord, that you care about all things concerning me, that you will heal my body and touch my mind. I thank you, Lord, that when I'm weak, you make me strong. I thank you, Father, that you are for me, not against me.

I thank you, Father, for your holy peace invading my life and my circumstances. I thank you for wisdom in this area where I need healing and strength. I thank you for giving me the ability to overcome anything that stands in the way of the greatness that you have planned for my life. In Jesus's name, amen.

CHAPTER 11

Racing to the Rescue

Commit to the Lord whatever you do,
and he will establish your plans.

— Proverbs 16:3

I was in the Upper Peninsula of Michigan, snowmobiling with some buddies. The conditions were perfect, with snow falling nonstop. Riding down trails—even blazing new ones—opens my mind.

I typically have random times of conversation with God. On this particular day, I was snowmobiling back to the cabin for the night, and a question popped into my head: How many encounters does it take for someone to get saved, go through healing and forgiveness, and bear fruit?

The Holy Spirit answered me before I was even done with the question. He said, "One encounter!" I began to laugh really hard. Excitement came over me. Here I was flying down a trail at sixty miles per hour, and the Holy Spirit was speaking to me. God is so cool.

I had more back-and-forth conversation with the Lord during that ride to the cabin, even setting up some possible scenarios as to how he might work with people I knew. Then I went to bed and forgot all about it.

This snowmobiling trip to the U.P. was an annual thing for over a decade. Sometimes I was with Christian buddies, other times quite the opposite. Then came a season in my life that was explosive with the blessings of God. I had submitted myself to Christ, so that he could flow through me and use me. I went up north with a great bunch of guys who cared for each other, and on the way home, one of them accepted Christ. God was on the move.

Spring of 2015 was for me a season of anticipation. I was awaiting the arrival of my very own purpose-built racecar. It was taking over a year to build. One day in late April, I received the phone call; the car was done. I dropped everything and went to pick it up.

It was a sunny seventy degrees here in Michigan when I drove the car home. Within ten hours, we had seven inches of heavy wet snow on the ground. Yes, this is spring in Michigan.

I was sad that I couldn't drive my new car that day. But I noticed something as I cut through the neighborhood in my truck. A beautiful black Corvette sat in a neighbor's driveway, covered with that heavy wet snow. I asked myself, how could someone leave such a car out in weather like this?

Five days later, with the weather cleared, I was coming home from a long day of running errands in my new racecar, and I noticed that black Corvette again in my neighbor's driveway. I felt a compelling nudge from the Holy Spirit to pull in and tell this guy he had a nice car. Very weird, I thought to myself.

I was on the phone with my grandma, so I kept driving. After telling her good-bye, I made a right instead of a left and circled the neighborhood. Random thoughts were coming into my head: I was tired, I had to go to the bathroom, and so on. But I had passed by this house for over two years, often waving at the man when he was in the yard. His corner house was beautiful, very well maintained, and he always seemed to be home. After circling the block, I pulled into his driveway.

I knocked on the man's door, and he came right out, introduced himself, and started looking at my car. I complimented him on his Corvette and told him I was his neighbor. I asked him if he would like to go for a quick ride to see the differences in our cars, and he said yes.

As we finished our little spin, this man invited me into his house for a minute. He wanted to tell me about an upcoming car show. I walked inside, and an interesting feeling came over me. I sensed a spirit of death. I had felt this before, but never like this.

I asked the Lord what the heck was going on. He answered me clear as day, "Today is the day of salvation." Wow, I thought, OK, what do you want me to do? I heard immediately in my heart, "Tell him the Easter story."

Within five minutes, the presence of Christ permeated this house, driving away the darkness. This man—I'll call him Mark—began weeping on my shoulder when I asked him if he wanted to accept the free gift of life that Christ died to give him. Mark said he was Jewish, and I told him that was not a problem; Jesus was Jewish too.

With tears flowing down his face, Mark said he had been trying to kill himself for over eight months but was continually unsuccessful. He had been crying out to God to take his life. The Lord answered his prayer in his kitchen on that sunny April day of 2015, but not in the way Mark had expected. God did take his life, with the promise to make it new.

> Here I am! I stand at the door and knock. If anyone hears my voice and opens the door, I will come in and eat with that person, and they with me.
>
> To the one who is victorious, I will give the right to sit with me on my throne, just as I was victorious and sat down with my Father on his throne. (Revelation 3:20–21)

As Mark's tears turned to tears of joy, I ministered to him there in his kitchen. The next few hours were crazy amazing. The Holy Spirit began to soften Mark's heart, touching areas of deep-rooted pain, bitterness, anger, hate, fear, torment, suicidal thoughts, helplessness, and hopelessness.

The Holy Spirit whispered to me, "One encounter. You asked how many, remember. Well, here it is in action."

The evening came to a close, and I headed home. Sarah had been calling me, so I told her I had been in the neighborhood, dealing with an amazing situation. That night I could barely sleep, I was so excited.

I continued to listen to the Holy Spirit concerning Mark. I wanted to keep myself open, to do whatever I could to help him come into the family of Christ. One prophetic word the Lord gave me for him—that the Lord wanted to give him the heart of a father—has allowed him to continue healing on a daily basis. We can't be pushy; we can only love.

Over the last year, Mark has blossomed into an amazing servant of the Lord. He started attending church and even comes to our men's Power Hour events. He is bearing good fruit for the Lord. Everywhere he goes, he gives people big hugs and tells them how thankful he is that God allowed him to live. Mark is living proof that one encounter with the Creator is all it takes to bring salvation.

It is amazing—and a big blessing to me—that the Lord can use even my "motorsports ministry" to start a conversation and win a soul. God uses everything to draw people into the kingdom. We have to walk in his ways with confidence, because the world is looking for us.

Please use the platform God gives you, because there are dying and helpless people out there whom God wants you to help. Ask the Holy Spirit to speak to you. It's not weird. He speaks to me in random thoughts and even in the middle of business transactions. He uses on-the-job training to show me how he operates. I ask him questions, and he teaches me.

I'm so thankful to serve a loving Father who is in constant pursuit of us when we don't deserve it. I know his voice as he speaks to my heart.

I will instruct you and teach you in the way you
should go;

I will counsel you with my loving eye on you.
(Psalm 32:8)

Pray that God will use you in mighty ways. And if you are
facing anything that doesn't align with the kingdom of heaven, ask Christ to battle on your behalf.

* * * * *

*Father, in the mighty name of Jesus, I give you glory,
honor, and praise. I thank you for the cross and the resurrection of Jesus. I thank you for the power of Christ
in my life every day.*

*Father, give me the ability to submit to the plans you
have for me. Give me the daily grace to walk in a way
that honors you. Show me those you want me to serve,
and give me your words for them. That all may come to
know you, in Jesus's name I pray, amen.*

The Best Prayer You'll Ever Pray

"I tell you the truth, unless you are born again, you cannot see the Kingdom of God."

— John 3:3, *NLT*

Perhaps you find yourself in Mark's position, lacking purpose or passion for life. Perhaps you have yet to ask Jesus Christ in your heart to be your Lord and Savior, your partner in it all. I would ask you to pray the best prayer you'll ever pray—the most powerful prayer you will find in this book. It is the prayer of salvation.

Being born again is a decision to relinquish your control over your life and to allow forgiveness into your heart. It is a healing that only God can do. Through the prayer of salvation, you acknowledge that you have sinned—fallen short—and you ask Christ into your heart. The result is fullness, wholeness: You are a new creation in Christ. "Therefore if any man *be* in Christ, *he is* a new creature: old things are passed away; behold, all things are made new" (2 Corinthians 5:17, *KJV*).

Being born again gives you "partnership with God" on this planet, and it also writes your name in the Lamb's book of life, promising you eternity with Christ. The moment you pray this prayer and start understanding Jesus's character, you have the opportunity to walk out your destiny. So please pray with me:

> *Father, I thank you for Jesus. I thank you that he died for my sins and rose again so that I can have life and life more abundantly. I repent of my sins, and I ask you to come into my heart and be my Lord, my Savior. I ask that you would walk with me all the days of my life. Allow your character to permeate my body, mind, spirit, and soul. In Jesus's name, I accept you. Amen.*

Many of you have been following God for some time. You have repented of your sins, and you truly strive to follow him every day. Perhaps you have a calling that needs some tweaking. People in this world are waiting for you and your unique message, which you alone can bring them. It is a message that will draw them into a true relationship with Christ, that will change them and break through anything standing in their way. Think about it: We all have the ability to launch someone into their great future with Christ.

How do we launch into a life of greater power, greater passion, and greater purpose? I believe we all need to talk to God in prayer. Our prayer can be as simple as a conversation with a friend. God is our friend. He is our Father. He desires to spend time with us every day.

It's good to have a particular time to meet with the Lord every day. It can also be helpful to meet him in a "secret place."

Your secret place can be a room in your home, a chapel, even your car. Or like me, you might pick your garage. It is any place where you can quiet your mind and focus on talking to God.

Ask the Lord questions. Tell him your greatest pains and frustrations. Share with him your greatest dreams. Invite him in. Ask him to give you the ability to listen with your heart and mind. He will speak to you.

Write down your requests. Find scriptures to go with them, so you can stand on God's promises about these requests. Hang them up where you can see them daily. Speak the prayers and scriptures out loud. Your faith will grow, and so will your relationship with and trust in the Lord.

If God is for you, NOTHING can be against you (see Romans 8:31). Bring the people and situations that matter to him.

Pray with your family, your colleagues, your employees and team members, and your friends. Watch God unlock your greatest dreams and launch you into a destiny of greatness in Christ! God cares about all things concerning you.

> Do not be anxious about anything, but in every situation, by prayer and petition, with thanksgiving, present your requests to God. And the peace of God, which transcends all understanding, will guard your hearts and your minds in Christ Jesus. (Philippians 4:6–7)

* * * * *

My prayer for you:

Lord, I pray for my friends reading this book. Give them peace that surpasses their own understanding. Guard their hearts and minds. Protect their dreams, and nurture them in wisdom, understanding, and truth.

I pray Psalm 91 and the blessings of Deuteronomy 28 over these readers' jobs, businesses, ministries, and homes. Bless them, Lord, I pray, in Jesus's name. Amen!